SingleFocus DEVOTIONAL

ASSURING
THE PROMISES
OF GOD

D.J. MARTIN

SingleFocus Ministry® Series

D.J. MARTIN

www.1singlefocus.wordpress.com
1singlefocus@gmail.com

Cover and Photography Created by D.J. Martin and L. Martin

DEVOTIONAL:

ASSURING THE PROMISES OF GOD

Copyrighted 2013

ALL RIGHTS RESERVED

ISBN: 978-0-9610182-0-7

Martin Publications

Printed in the United States of America

To my sister, Annette Lewis, who tirelessly focuses on her God-given purpose of administering God's loving kindness (Romans 12:8 &13).

I count not myself to have [achieved]: but this one thing I do, forgetting those things which are behind, and [focus] on those things which are before, I press toward the mark for the prize of the high calling of God in Christ Jesus. PHILIPPIANS 3:13-14

Table of Contents

FOCUS
Introduction 6

FOCUS 1
His Will & Purpose 9

FOCUS 2
Speak Truth 17

FOCUS 3
Get Wisdom 25

FOCUS 4
Be Strong and Courageous 32

FOCUS 5
Flee Idolatry..39

FOCUS 6
Avoid Pride..48

FOCUS 7
Obey God...55

FOCUS 8
Give 63

FOCUS 9
Hope in God 72

FOCUS 10
Forgive 79

FOCUS 11
Choose LIFE 86

FOCUS 12
Assure the Promises of God 97

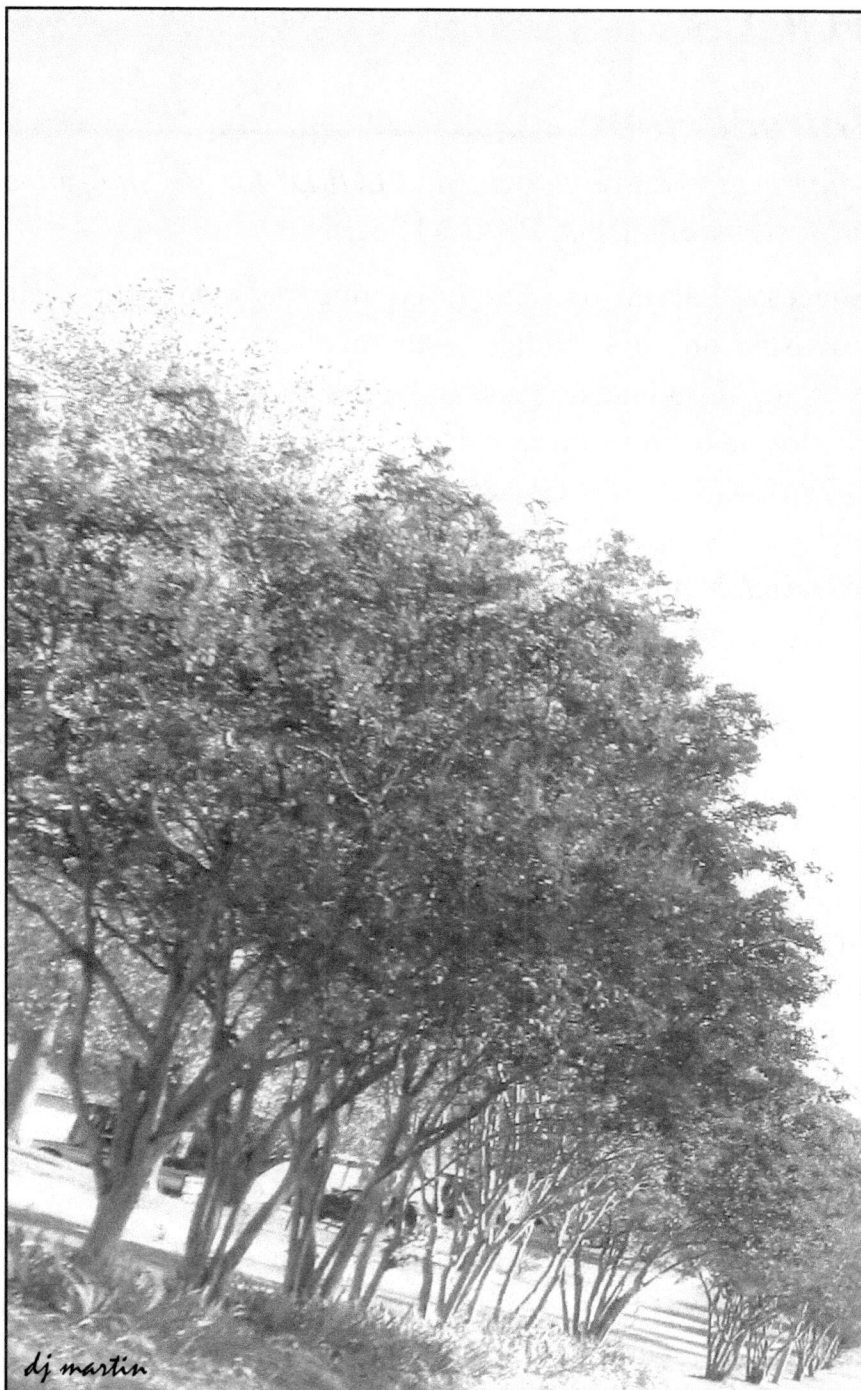

dj martin

5

FOCUS

*Introduction*_____

Mine eyes are ever toward the LORD; for He shall pluck my feet out of the net. PSALM 25:15

Successful living is *acutely* contingent upon your focus. Focusing on your studies, your practice time or your networking is advantageous and good to do, however you cannot have true success, if your first focus is not on the LORD. This Devotional is designed to sharpen your focus and inspire you to actively seek God's will; sequentially assuring the promises of God.

Quality devotional time should be experiential and spiritually maturing. As you study, you will become not only a hearer and prayer of the word, but also a doer of the word. Expect to be progressively encouraged and to fervently grow more intimate with God as you consistently meditate and walk in the Scriptures. Most assuredly you will begin focusing on God's agenda and attain new spiritual heights. His will and His purpose for your life will become your focus and pursuit. Your perception of matters from God's perspective will give you clear vision. New insight will stimulate your personal desire to accomplish His will and proliferate experiencing the promises of God triumphantly.

Keep a journal or a notebook, as you read and meditate on the Scriptures, to record your thoughts and document your application of the 'Focus' points and how you experience

God and His promises in your earnest prayerful daily walk with Him. Chronicling your acute devotional journey will help you to judiciously appraise your spiritual growth and your intimate relationship with God.

Undoubtedly, your increasing spiritual maturity will assure the vibrant discernment of your divine purpose. Doing the will of God for His glory will perpetually become your 'Single Focus'

dj martin

FOCUS 1

*His Will & Purpose*_____

God's Concern

- ISAIAH 1:2 *Hear, O heavens, and give ear, O earth: for the LORD has spoken, "I have nourished and brought up children, and they have rebelled against Me."*

- ISAIAH 1:4 *Ah sinful nation, a people laden with iniquity, a seed of evildoers, children that are corrupters: they have forsaken the LORD, they have provoked the Holy One of Israel unto anger, they are gone away backward.*

- ISAIAH 1:11-14 *"To what purpose is the multitude of your sacrifices unto Me?" saith the LORD: "I am full of the burnt offerings of rams and the fat of fed beasts; and I delight not in the blood of bullocks, or of lambs, or of he goats.*

  When ye come to appear before Me, who hath required this at your hand, to tread My courts?

  Bring no more vain [offerings]; incense is an abomination unto Me; the new moons and Sabbaths, the calling of assemblies, I cannot away with; it is iniquity, even the solemn meeting.

Your new moons and your appointed feasts My soul [hates]: they are a trouble unto Me; I am weary to bear them."

God's Response

- ISAIAH 1:7 *Your country is desolate; your cities are burned with fire: your land, strangers devour it in your presence, and it is desolate, as overthrown by strangers.*

- ISAIAH 1:15 *...When ye spread forth your hands, I will hide Mine eyes from you: yea, when ye make many prayers, I will not hear: your hands are full of blood.*

- ISAIAH 1:18-20 *"Come now, and let us reason together", saith the LORD: "though your sins be as scarlet, they shall be as white as snow; though they be red like crimson, they shall be as wool.*

  If ye be willing and obedient, ye shall eat the good of the land: But if ye refuse and rebel, ye shall be devoured with the sword:" for the mouth of the LORD hath spoken it.

God's Will

- PSALM 26:2 *Examine me, O LORD, and prove me; try my reins and my heart.*

- ISAIAH 1:16-17 *Wash you, make you clean; put away the evil of your doings from before Mine eyes; cease to do evil; Learn to do well; seek judgment, relieve the oppressed, judge the fatherless, [and] plead for the widow.*

- MATTHEW 22:37 *Jesus said unto him, "Thou shalt Love the Lord thy God with all thy heart, and with all thy soul, and with all thy mind."*

- JOHN 4:34 *Jesus said unto them, "My meat is to do the will of Him that sent Me, and to finish His work."*

- 2THESSALONIANS 1:11-12 *Wherefore we also pray always for you, that our God would count you worthy of this calling, and fulfill all the good pleasure of His goodness and the work of faith with power: that the name of our Lord Jesus Christ may be glorified in you and you in Him, according to the grace of our God and the Lord Jesus Christ.*

Too many of us allow sin to be a coat that we wear during the week then we simply change to a pious coat on Sunday morning. No matter how we dress or the uniform we wear, God recognizes sinful hearts. Some of the things we do routinely or we have gotten in a habit of doing may seem insignificant but is sinful disobedience in God's sight. Let us not allow attending church or worshipping Christ to be merely a postscript of our lives.

Sometimes sin can become so much a part of our lifestyle that we fail to recognize it and/or fail to repent. Therefore we show up at worship and all the singing, all the lifting up of hands toward heaven; and all the giving is an exercise in futility, because God's anger has been kindled against us. That is the reason we should regularly come before God allowing Him to reveal sin in our lives and give us a way of escape from continuing to walk in trespasses against Him.

Be careful to not become like the people in the book of Isaiah. The children of God were doing the routine. They were caught up in the customs of the day and had begun to disregard the Holiness of God. They had begun to treat Him as if He was average and ordinary. They came to Him with average, ordinary or blemished offerings. They had their feasts and holidays, but their hearts and minds were dastardly wicked. Sin and disrespect for the statutes of God was their lifestyle. So they went to the temple and had their feasts, thinking nothing was wrong, until eventually God's patience had worn thin.

Admittedly, we tend to see sin in other people's lives well before we see sin in our own lives. Like the people in the book of Isaiah, we can get comfortable in our lifestyle even though it can be as dirty as Linus' security blanket. That is why we must consistently examine ourselves.

Truly there is no condemnation for those who are in Christ Jesus. When we examine ourselves the desired results is not to cover ourselves in a cloak of guilt and shame, but to confess it (acknowledge to God that we have been wrong), repent and turn or refrain from the practice of it. It is also to allow us to *genuinely* experience God's forgiveness, healing, restoration, presence, fellowship, power, love, mercy and grace. It is then that God will faithfully reveal to us, perpetuate and empower us to obey His will and purpose for our lives.

Though we face uncertainty and challenges each new day, let us resolve to examine ourselves and put away sinful disobedience so that we can diligently do the work, which God has called us to do. We must allow the Holy Spirit to help us to focus on His will and purpose for our lives.

As we focus on God's will and purpose, surely each new day will bring appreciation for the powerful movement of God in our daily lives. Keeping our spiritual eyes focused on His will and purpose enhances the experiencing of the delivering, providing, forgiving, healing and victorious grace, mercy and power of our LORD and Savior, Jesus Christ!

"Search me, O God, and know my heart: try me, and know my thoughts: and see if there [is] any wicked way in me, and lead me in the way everlasting."
PSALM 139:23-24

Reflection

1. Do you desire to walk in God's will and purpose?

2. How has the Spirit helped you walk in God's will?

3. Do you allow God to reveal sin in your life?

4. Do you have a habit that is contrary to God's will?

5. How did God reveal it to you?

6. Have you observed the consequences of rebellious behavior?

7. How do you keep from repeating the thing(s) God has confronted you about?

8. What Scripture(s) help you stay in God's will?

9. Have you recently experienced benefits from doing God's will?

dj martin

16

FOCUS 2

Speak Truth————————————————

God's Concern

- PSALM 52:1-4 *Why boasts thou thyself in mischief, O mighty man? The goodness of God endures continually.*

  Thy tongue devises mischiefs; like a sharp razor, working deceitfully. You love evil more than good; and lying rather than to speak righteousness. You love all devouring words, O thou deceitful tongue.

- JEREMIAH 9:8 *Their tongue is as an arrow shot out; it speaketh deceit: one speaketh peaceably to his neighbor with his mouth, but in heart he layeth his wait.*

- JAMES 3:10 *Out of the same mouth proceeds blessing and cursing. My brethren, these things ought not so to be.*

God's Response

- PSALM 52:5-6 *God shall likewise destroy thee for-ever, He shall take thee away, and pluck thee out of thy dwelling place, and root thee out of the land of the living.*

  The righteous also shall see and fear, and shall laugh at him: "Lo this is the man that made not God his strength; but trusted in the abundance of his riches, and strengthened himself in his wickedness."

- ISAIAH 9:16 *...The leaders of this people cause them to err; and they that are led of them are destroyed.*

- ISAIAH 9:17 *Therefore the Lord shall have no joy in their young men; neither shall have mercy on their fatherless and widows: for every one is a hypocrite and an evildoer, and every mouth speaks folly. For all this His anger is not turned away, but His hand is stretched out still.*

- LUKE 21:15 *I will give you a mouth and wisdom, which all your adversaries will not be able to refute nor resist.*

God's Will

- PSALM 44:8 *In God we boast all the day long, and praise Thy name forever.*

- PSALM 47:6 *Sing praises to God, sing praises: sing praises unto our King, sing praises.*

- PSALM 47:7 *For God is the King of all the earth; sing ye praises with understanding.*

- PSALM 48:1 *Great is the LORD, and greatly to be praised in the city of our God, in the mountain of His holiness.*

- PSALM 48:14 *For this God is our God forever and ever; He will be our guide even unto death.*

- PSALM 52:8-9 *But I am like a green olive tree in the house of God: I trust in the mercy of God forever and ever.*

  I will praise Thee forever, because Thou hast done it: and I will wait on Thy name; for it is good before Thy saints.

- PSALM 145:21 *My mouth shall speak the praise of the LORD: and let all flesh bless His holy name forever and ever.*

- PROVERBS 4:24 *Put away from thee a [deceitful] mouth, and perverse lips put far from thee.*

- PROVERBS 8:13 *The fear of the LORD is to hate evil: pride, and arrogancy, and the evil way, and the forward mouth, do I hate.*

- PROVERBS 21:23 *Whoso keepeth his mouth and his tongue, keepeth his soul from troubles.*

- ECCLESIASTES 5:2 *Be not [quick] with [your] mouth, Let not [your] heart be hasty to utter anything before God:*
  God is in heaven and [you] upon earth: therefore, let [your] words be few.

- MATTHEW 4:4 *...But He answered and said, "It is written, Man shall not live by bread alone, but by every word that proceeds out of the mouth of God."*

- EPHESIANS 4:14-15 *That we henceforth be no more children, tossed to and fro, and carried about with every wind of doctrine, by the sleight of men, and cunning craftiness, whereby they lie in wait to deceive; But speaking the truth in love, may grow up into Him in all things, which is the head, even Christ...*

- EPHESIANS 4:22-25 *Put off concerning the former conversation, the old man, which is corrupt according to the deceitful lusts; and be renewed in the spirit of your mind; and that ye put on the new man, which after God is created in righteousness and true holiness.*

  Wherefore putting away lying, speak every man truth with his neighbor: for we are members one of another.

- EPHESIANS 4:27 *Neither give place to the devil.*

- EPHESIANS 4:29 *Let no corrupt communication proceed out of your mouth, but that which is good to the use of edifying, that it may minister grace unto the hearers.*

- EPHESIANS 4:31 *Let all bitterness, and wrath, and anger, and clamor, and evil speaking, be put away from you, with all malice.*

- 2THESSALONIANS 1:12 *...That the name of our Lord Jesus Christ may be glorified in you and [you]* *in Him, according to the grace of our God and the Lord Jesus Christ.*

- JAMES 3:13 *Who is a wise man and endued with knowledge among you? Let him [show] out of a good conversation his works with meekness of wisdom.*

Regrettably, this generation has seen a great escalation of lying tongues from ungodly leaders (including their allies) *and* godly leaders (including the un-questioning members of their churches). God is not only concerned with willful deceitful tongues of leaders, but He is also very concerned about each person, individually; He is concerned about what proceeds out of the mouth of the solitary person. This mighty God is a personal God, intimately concerned about the individual and their personal singular growth. Taking His correction is good for the body and soul. Surely God's stern warning about guarding the tongue must be taken very seriously. Discernment must consistently be prayed for, because the wicked is inherently cunning and artfully deceiving.

Remember the infamous conversation in the Garden of Eden? The whole earth was served notice that this will be the plan of attack: cunning and deceitful words from the devil. Adam and Eve were astutely deceived and believed a lie, because of the devil's cleverly crafted words.

Let us resolve to be careful who we hang out with and whose words we hear or we may not only believe a lie, but we will become disciples of liars and repeat their lies, even to our children.

We should test the words of our various acquaintances, our leaders, and our own lips to see how the words measure up to the Word of God. We must guard our tongues so as not to deceive or slander men nor diminish their spirit with our words. Our focus should be on using our lips to praise God, speak truth, extend grace and encourage others.

Let our conversation be in love; speaking words of truth, which is His Word; and glorifying and praising God daily! May this resolve bring to our lives: evidence of praises to God; ever-increasing appetite for His Word; and lordship of Jesus Christ over our tongues.

As we plant seeds of blessings, grace, righteousness and truth with our mouths, may we reap bountifully the same in return (Luke 6:38).

"Set a watch, O LORD, before my mouth; keep the door of my lips." PSALM 141:3

Reflection

1. Do your words reflect truth?

2. Do you often speak encouraging words?

3. Do your words reflect the love of Christ?

4. Have you recently been deceived?

5. Who do you hear often speaking words of deceit?

6. Who do you hear degrading and discouraging others?

7. Who do you trust to tell the truth?

8. Do you believe it is the truth, because: you agree; you know it to be fact; or it lines up with the Word of God?

9. Do you test the words of leaders with the Word of God?

10. Has God ever revealed the truth just before someone approached you with an attempt to deceive?

11. How do you identify truth from fiction?

12. What scripture(s) help you guard your tongue?

L. Martin

FOCUS 3

Get Wisdom

God's Concern

- JEREMIAH 4:22 ...*My people is foolish, they have not known Me; they are [silly] children and they have none understanding: they are wise to do evil, but to do good they have no knowledge.*

God's Response

- PROVERBS 3:35 *The wise shall inherit glory: but shame shall be the promotion of fools.*

- PROVERBS 13:20 *He that walks with wise men shall be wise: but a companion of fools shall be destroyed.*

- PROVERBS 14:3 *In the mouth of the foolish is a rod of pride: but the lips of the wise shall preserve them.*

- PROVERBS 19:29 ...*Judgments are prepared for scorners and stripes for the back of fools.*

God's Will

- PROVERBS 1:7 ...*The fear of the LORD is the beginning of knowledge: but fools despise wisdom and instruction.*

- PROVERBS 2:2 *Incline thine ear unto wisdom, and apply thine heart to understanding.*

- PROVERBS 3:1-2 *Forget not My law; but let [your] heart keep My commandments: for length of days, and long life, and peace shall they add to [you].*

- PROVERBS 3:3 *Let not mercy and truth forsake thee: bind them about thy neck; write them upon the table of thine heart...*

- PROVERBS 3:5 *Trust in the LORD with all thine heart; and lean not unto thine own understanding.*

- PROVERBS 3:6 *In all [your] ways acknowledge Him, and He shall direct [your] paths.*

- PROVERBS 3:7 *Be not wise in thine own eyes: fear the LORD, and depart from evil.*

- PROVERBS 3:21 *Keep sound wisdom and discretion...*

- PROVERBS 3:31 *Envy thou not the oppressor, and choose none of his ways.*

- PROVERBS 4:5 *Get wisdom, get understanding: forget it not; neither decline from the words of my mouth.*

- PROVERBS 4:7 *...Wisdom is the principal thing; therefore get wisdom: and with all thy getting get understanding.*

- PROVERBS 4:13 *Take fast hold of instruction; let her not go: keep her; for she is thy life.*

- PROVERBS 4:14 *Enter not into the path of the wicked, and go not in the way of evil men.*

- PROVERBS 15:14 *...The heart of him that hath understanding seeketh knowledge: but the mouth of fools feedeth on foolishness.*

- MATTHEW 4:4 *Man shall not live by bread alone, but by every word that proceeds out of the mouth of God.*

- EPHESIANS 4:14 *That we henceforth be no more children, tossed to and fro, and carried about with every wind of doctrine, by the sleight of men, and cunning craftiness, whereby they lie in wait to deceive.*

- COLOSSIANS 3:16 *Let the word of Christ dwell in you richly in all wisdom; teaching and admonishing one another in PSALM and hymns and spiritual songs, singing with grace in your hearts to the Lord.*

- COLOSSIANS 4:5 *Walk in wisdom.*

- 2TIMOTHY 2:7 *Consider what I say; and the Lord give thee understanding in all things.*

- JAMES 3:13 *Who is a wise man and endued with knowledge among you? Let him show out of a good conversation his works with meekness of wisdom.*

This new century has ushered into the world a heavy cloud of cunning men who have so tenaciously crafted their words that foolishness and perversion of the Word of God has been believed and espoused by many, even those called by His name. Evil men have so cleverly disguised their words that it has become difficult to distinguish sound doctrine from foolishness.

We must innately hide the Word of God in our hearts so that we can accurately and judiciously distinguish wisdom from errant foolishness. We can determinedly avoid falling prey to cunning deception, if wisdom and understanding is our assiduous pursuit.

Like vigorously pursuing riches, seek wisdom from God with all diligence and strength. Pursue wisdom, knowledge and understanding as if it were more precious than gold or diamonds, because it is!

"...Wisdom is better than rubies; and all the things that may be desired are not to be compared to it."
Proverbs 8:11

May each new day bring wisdom and understanding so that we will not be the *'punch line'* of the devil's 'cruel comedy routine'; and be counted among the wicked and foolish by God.

Focus on experiencing ever increasing victory, because you lean not to your own understanding. In all your ways strive to acknowledge God, and fervently read His Word aggressively seeking "To know wisdom and instruction; to perceive the words of understanding (Proverbs 1:2)."

"If any of you lack wisdom, let him ask of God, that gives to all men liberally, and scolded not; and it shall be given him." JAMES 1:5

Reflection

1. Do you struggle with wisdom?

2. Do you daily seek wisdom and understanding from God?

3. Who do you trust to give you wise counsel?

4. Do you have difficulty making decisions?

5. Have you been discouraged by acting on foolish advice?

6. Why did you think their foolishness was wise advice?

7. Do you test the wisdom of others with the Word of God?

8. Have you recently experienced the wisdom of God?

9. How do you distinguish wisdom from foolishness?

10. What Scripture(s) help you walk in wisdom and avoid foolishness?

dj martin

FOCUS 4

Be Strong and Courageous ———————

God's Concern

- JEREMIAH 30:5 *For thus said the LORD; "We have heard a voice of trembling, of fear, and not of peace."*

- MARK 4:40 *...And He said unto them, "Why are ye so fearful? How is it that ye have no faith?"*

- JOHN 7:13 *Howbeit no man spoke openly of Him for fear of the Jews.*

God's Response

- PROVERBS 29:25 *The fear of man bringeth a snare: but whoso putteth his trust in the LORD shall be safe.*

- MARK 4:41 *...And they feared exceedingly, and said one to another, "What manner of man is this, that even the wind and the sea obey Him?"*

- ACTS 4:29 *...Lord, behold their threatening's: and grant unto Thy servants, that with all boldness they may speak Thy word.*

- ACTS 4:31 *And when they had prayed, the place was shaken where they were assembled together;*

and they were all filled with the Holy Ghost, and they spake the Word of God with boldness.

God's Will

- GENESIS 15:1 *After these things the word of the LORD came unto Abram in a vision, saying, "Fear not, Abram: I am thy shield, and thy exceeding great reward."*

- JOSHUA 1:9 *Have not I commanded thee? Be strong and of a good courage; be not afraid, neither be thou dismayed: for the LORD thy God is with thee whithersoever thou [go].*

- PSALM 118:6 *The LORD is on my side; I will not fear: what can man do unto me?*

- PROVERBS 9:10 *The fear of the LORD is the beginning of wisdom: and the knowledge of the holy is understanding.*

- JEREMIAH 1:8 *"Be not afraid of their faces: for I am with thee to deliver thee," saith the LORD.*

- PHILIPPIANS 1:14 *...And many of the brethren in the Lord, waxing confident by my bonds, are much more bold to speak the Word without fear.*

- HEBREW 13:6 *That we may boldly say, "The Lord is my helper, and I will not fear what man shall do unto me."*

Is there any doubt? Better yet, is there any fear? Daily the wicked and blind followers of demonic doctrines boldly wave their fists at God, declaring that His Word and true righteousness is not relevant. Deceivers ridicule and twist *'Truth and Righteousness'* without shame. Governments are boldly declaring, at every opportunity, that the Word of God is not expedient for their ungodly agenda. Adultery and Idolatry is the envy of even God's *'very elect.'* Rest assured that *All* wicked and wickedness have a destiny of defeat and destruction, because regardless of how the world tries to make it appear otherwise, God is greater than them all. He is God and there is no one in heaven or earth greater than He.

God is calling His children to start sounding the alarm without fear of man. No doubt, many have been called to proclaim the truth of God's word and His redemptive grace and mercy, but because of the nature of wickedness in high places, the depravity of men and foolish doctrine of their family, friends and acquaintances, they are fearful to speak the truth. God is encouraging the followers of Christ to not be afraid, but be strong and courageous. He is calling on His children to boldly speak deliverance to the captive and sight to the blind (Luke 4:18).

Look at the parable of the seeds in Mark 4. Christ tells us that if we sow seeds, there could be a growth in some that might multiply; the ones sown on good ground, those who hear the Word, accept it, and bear fruit: some thirtyfold, some sixty, and some a hundred (Mark 4:20). We who have accepted His Word are capable of bearing fruit: some thirtyfold, some sixty and some a hundred.

It is clear what the seeds planted by deceivers and warriors against *'Truth and Righteousness'* have produced. That's why, since the resurrection of Christ, the devil has tried to silence the saints of God through fear, ridicule and hateful intimidation; because if the righteous sow seeds, surely something good and righteous is going to grow.

To be strong and courageous in this generation is indeed a challenging command. God even had to say it at least three times to Joshua (Joshua 1: 6, 7, 9), because the battle is against a giant and intimidating opponent. The only way to not fear men is to grow in confidence that God is totally present and will crush all opposition.

Knowing that God should be feared much more than man; we can diligently sow seeds by boldly proclaiming truth. Our trust is in Him, our Rock, for He is almighty and all powerful; surrounding us with His presence; protecting us, and shielding us from our enemies.

Let us earnestly resolve to fear God and see "… one chase a thousand, and two put ten thousand to flight, [*as*] the Rock has sold them, and the LORD has shut them up (Deuteronomy 32:30)." Being filled with the Holy Spirit, with growing confidence in God, we can courageously use our gifts to vigorously proclaim the Word of God; boldly champion; and relentlessly propagate the truth of Christ and His righteousness.

"Finally, my brethren, be strong in the Lord, and in the power of His might." EPHESIANS 6:10

Reflection

1. Do you struggle with sharing the Gospel?

2. Are you intimidated by wicked voices?

3. What frightens you about sharing the truth about God?

4. What discourages you from revealing wickedness?

5. What Biblical figure(s) witnessed while under an ungodly government?

6. How did God protect and provide for them?

7. Do you disciple your children?

8. Do your co-workers know that you are a Christian?

9. Have you recently had the opportunity to expose un-righteousness and reveal righteousness?

10. Did you?

11. Has God given you a task and a purpose?

12. Does fear cause you to hesitate?

13. Who/what discourages you from doing God's will?

14. Who/what encourages you to do God's will?

15. What Scripture(s) help you to boldly obey God's will?

dj martin

FOCUS 5

*Flee Idolatry*_____

God's Concern

- 2KINGS 17:11-12 *There they burnt incense in all the high places, as did the heathen whom the LORD carried away before them; and wrought wicked things to provoke the LORD to anger. For they served idols, [of which] the LORD had said to them, "[You] shall not do this thing."*

- 2KINGS 17:14 *Notwithstanding they would not hear, but hardened their necks, like to the neck of their fathers, that did not believe in the LORD their God.*

- 1CHRONICLES 16:26 *For all the gods of the people are idols: but the LORD made the heavens.*

- PSALM 96:5 *For all the gods of the nations are idols: but the LORD made the heavens.*

- PSALM 106:36 *They served their idols: which were a snare unto them.*

- PSALM 106:38 *...And shed innocent blood, even the blood of their sons and of their daughters, whom they sacrificed unto the idols...: and the land was polluted with blood.*

- PSALM 106:39 *Thus were they defiled with their own works, and went a whoring with their own inventions.*

- PSALM 115:4 *Their idols are silver and gold, the work of men's hands.*

- PROVERBS 5:21...*The ways of man are before the eyes of the LORD and He ponders all his goings.*

- EZEKIEL 14:3 *Son of man, these men have set up their idols in their heart, and put the stumbling block of their iniquity before their face.*

- EZEKIEL 23:39 ...*For when they had slain their children to their idols, then they came the same day into My sanctuary to profane it; and, lo, thus have they done in the midst of Mine house.*

God's Response

- GENESIS 15:1 *I am thy shield, and thy exceeding great reward.*

- DEUTERONOMY 28:20 *The LORD shall send upon thee cursing, vexation, and rebuke, in all that thou settest thine hand unto for to do, until thou be destroyed, and until thou perish quickly; because of the wickedness of thy doings, whereby thou hast forsaken Me.*

- PSALM 18:31 *For who is God save the LORD? Or who is a rock save our God?*

- PSALM 95:3 *For the LORD is a great God and a great King above all gods.*

- EZEKIEL 37:23 *Neither shall they defile themselves any more with their idols, nor with their detestable things, nor with any of their transgressions: but I will save them out of all their dwelling places, wherein they have sinned, and will cleanse them: so shall they be My people, and I will be their God.*

- COLOSSIANS 3:5-6 *Mortify therefore your members which are upon the earth; fornication, un- cleanness, inordinate affection, evil concupiscence, and covetousness, which is idolatry: For which things' sake the wrath of God cometh on the children of disobedience...*

God's Will

- EXODUS 20:3 *Thou shalt have no other gods before Me.*

- LEVITICUS 19:4 *Turn ye not unto idols, nor make to yourselves molten gods: I am the LORD your God.*

- 1CHRONICLES 16:25 *For great is the LORD, and greatly to be praised: He also is to be feared above all gods.*

- PSALM 29:2 *Give unto the LORD the glory due unto His name; worship the LORD in the beauty of holiness.*

- PSALM 118:8 *It is better to trust in the LORD than to put confidence in man.*

- PSALM 118:9 *It is better to trust in the LORD than to put confidence in princes.*

- ISAIAH 31:7 *Every man shall cast away his idols of silver, and his idols of gold, which your own hands have made unto you for a sin.*

- MATTHEW 6:32-33 *Your heavenly Father knows that ye have need of all these things... Seek ye first the kingdom of God, and His righteousness; and all these things shall be added unto you.*

- LUKE 4:8 *[You] shall worship the LORD your God and Him only [you] shall serve.*

- 1CORINTHIANS 10:14...*Flee from idolatry.*

- 1CORINTHIANS 10:31...*Whether therefore ye eat or drink, or [whatever] ye do, do it all to the glory of God.*

- COLOSSIANS 3:1 *If [you] then be risen with Christ, seek those things which are above, where Christ sitteth on the right hand of God.*

- COLOSSIANS 3:2 *Set your affection on things above, not on things on the earth.*

- COLOSSIANS 3:17 *And [whatever you] do in word or deed: do all in the name of the Lord Jesus, giving thanks to God and the Father by Him.*

- COLOSSIANS 3:23 *And whatsoever ye do, do it heartily, as to the Lord and not to men...*

- 1THESSALONIANS 1:9 *For they themselves shew of us what manner of entering in we had unto you, and how ye turned to God from idols to serve the living and true God.*

- 1JOHN 5:21 *Little children, keep yourselves from idols. Amen.*

It is imperative that we analyze ourselves. We can easily slip into idolatry when we take our eyes off of Christ, our source, and focus on His resources, which are made available to us at the command and favor of God.

I remember working so much overtime, because of the money, that I lost focus on doing the kingdom work God had called me to do. I was so focused on the money, that I was too tired to do the work of the Lord. One morning, I looked at my W2 Tax form and discovered that all my overtime work was paying homage to the government; the harder I worked, the more the government took. My job and the money had become my idol. I didn't go into it thinking, "I'm no longer trusting in God, I'm going to trust in silver and gold," I slowly slipped into idolatry.

Idolatry comes in all forms: people (living or dead), rulers, government, leaders, job, silver, gold, nature, food, rituals, philosophies, animals, race, gender, religion, traditions, sports, carvings, charms, body, habits, immorality, etc. Is there something or someone you are more passionate about or more focused on then the Lord Jesus Christ, who was so passionate about His love for all mankind that He died a violent and humiliating death for the redemption of sin?

Seriously think about it! Are you depending on actors, movies, music, entertainment, immorality, drugs or alcohol to give you joy? Are you depending on the government to feed you, clothe you, and/or heal you? Are you depending on the work of your hands, your giving or doing good deeds to receive forgiveness? Are you depending on your job, politicians, your spouse or your children to give you security? Are you depending on your pastor, your church, your denomination, your horoscope, your psychic, your tradition or your rituals to give you hope and a future? Are you more passionate about buying a car or a house then about developing your relationship with God? Does someone saying something derogatory about your friend, lover or mother; something insulting about your leader, your pastor, your boss or your mentor offend you more than you take offence if someone says something offensive about Christ and/or His Word?

Someone (may have been my pastor) said that "We make time for what we put first or care most about." I also say,

"When you see what someone is most passionate about, you see who or what they worship."

Unfortunately, many people have idols in their lives. They think that because they go to Church every Sabbath, they aren't idolaters, but God sees that they give more time and glory to other things and people than they do Him.

This is crucial and demands our urgent consideration. God is not pleased about idolatry. We must indeed consistently examine ourselves and be careful to flee idolatry, where and when we find ourselves to be idolaters. Become more passionate about glorifying God and acknowledge that there is none greater than He. He alone is our Savior. He is God and no one in heaven or earth is greater than Him.

Be thankful to God and focus on Him as the source for health, joy, security, hope and prosperity. Put no other gods before Him. Love God with all your heart, mind and strength. Worship God and Him only, for He is LORD and He provides all that we need! HE IS GOD ALONE!

"Wherefore, my dearly beloved, flee from idolatry."
1CORINTHIANS 10:14

Reflection

1. What/who have you observed becoming idols?

2. What/who do you think is an idol?

3. What Scriptures show what God thinks about idols?

4. Is there anyone or anything you put before God?

5. If you find idolatry in your own life, what will you do?

6. What Scripture(s) are helpful to avoid idolatry?

dj martin

FOCUS 6

Avoid Pride————————————————

God's Concern

- PSALM 10:4 *The wicked, through the pride of his countenance, will not seek after God: God is not in all his thoughts.*

- PROVERBS 6:16-19 *These six things the LORD hates, yea, seven are an abomination to Him:*
  1. *A proud look,*
  2. *A lying tongue,*
  3. *And hands that shed innocent blood,*
  4. *An heart that devises wicked imaginations,*
  5. *Feet that be swift in running to mischief,*
  6. *A false witness who speaks lies and he that sows discord among brethren.*

- 1JOHN 2:16 *All that is in the world:*
  1. *The lust of the flesh,*
  2. *The lust of the eyes,*
  3. *and the pride of life;*
     is not of the Father, but is of the world.

God's Response

- 2CHRONICLES 7:14 *If My people, which are called by My name, shall humble themselves, and pray, and seek My face, and turn from their wicked ways; then will I hear from heaven, and will forgive their sin, and will heal their land.*

- PROVERBS 11:2 *When pride cometh, then cometh shame: but with the lowly is wisdom.*

- PROVERBS 16:5 *Everyone that is proud in heart is an abomination to the LORD; though hand join in hand, he shall not be unpunished.*

- PROVERBS 16:18 *Pride goes before destruction and a haughty spirit before a fall.*

- PROVERBS 29:23 *A man's pride shall bring him low: but honor shall uphold the humble in spirit.*

- ISAIAH 23:9 *The LORD of hosts hath purposed it, to stain the pride of all glory, and to bring into contempt all the honorable of the earth.*

- JEREMIAH 13:17 *But if ye will not hear it, my soul shall weep in secret places for your pride; and mine eye shall weep sore, and run down with tears, because the LORD'S flock is carried away captive.*

- JEREMIAH 50:31 *"Behold, I am against thee, O thou most proud," saith the Lord GOD of hosts: "for thy day is come, the time that I will visit thee."*

- JEREMIAH 50:32 *And the most proud shall stumble and fall, and none shall raise him up: and I will kindle a fire in his cities, and it shall devour all round about him.*

- MATTHEW 23:12 *And whosoever shall exalt himself shall be abased; and he that shall humble himself shall be exalted.*

- JAMES 4:6 *God resists the proud, but gives grace to the humble.*

God's Will

- 1CHRONICLES 16:24-25 *Declare His glory among the heathen; His marvelous works among all nations. For great is the LORD, and greatly to be praised: He also is to be feared above all gods.*

- PSALM 29:2 *Give unto the LORD the glory due unto His name; worship the LORD in the beauty of holiness.*

- PSALM 34:2 *My soul shall make her boast in the LORD; the humble shall hear thereof and be glad.*

- PSALM 44:8 *In God we boast all the day long, and praise Thy name forever.*

- JEREMIAH 13:15 *Hear ye, and give ear; be not proud: for the LORD hath spoken.*

- 1CORINTHIANS 6:20 *For [you] are bought with a price: therefore glorify God in your body, and in your spirit, which are God's.*

- COLOSSIANS 3:17 *And [whatever] ye do in word or deed, do all in the name of the Lord Jesus, giving thanks to God the Father by Him.*

- COLOSSIANS 3:23 *And [whatever] ye do, do it heartily, as to the Lord and not to men...*

- JAMES 4:10 *Humble yourselves in the sight of the Lord, and He shall lift you up.*

- 1PETER 5:6 *Humble yourselves therefore under the mighty hand of God, that He may exalt you in due time.*

Resist pride and flee from the company of the proud. We must humble ourselves and allow Christ to be our Lord. Whatever we excel in, we need to remember that the gifts and abilities we have are all from God. Whatever good we do should be for the glory of God, not for the gratification of our ego. We should refrain from boasting in ourselves or our abilities. We ought not to think more highly of ourselves than others (Romans 12:3). It is God that gives the air that we breathe and the skills, talents and abilities that we exhibit. He deserves the greater applause.

Some boast in their riches, families, houses, talents, skills, churches, groups, vehicles, wardrobes, education, position or status, etc. But it is essential that the children of God be ever mindful that God is the source of all that they are and all that they have. He can take it away in an instant, if they continue in pride and do not humble themselves.

Knowing that God hates pride, do not let pride keep you from fellowship with God, your friends and love ones. Sometimes having too much pride to say, "I'm sorry" or "I forgive you" tears a family apart, and divorce lawyers are outpacing the undertakers in prosperity.

Walk in humility. Boast in the Lord, acknowledging and glorifying Him for every great accomplishment and every good work. With the ever present help of the Holy Spirit, judiciously resolve to pull off pride and put on humility. Give God the honor, glory and praise due Him. Always seek to point all eyes toward God.

"Better it is to be of an humble spirit with the lowly, than to divide the spoil with the proud." PROVERBS 16:19

Reflection

1. Have you observed pride?

2. What forms of pride have you observed?

3. What leaders exhibit pride and arrogance?

4. Who do you know that has a spirit of pride?

5. What Scriptures show what God thinks about pride?

6. What do you think pride is?

7. If you find pride in your own life, what will you do?

8. What Scripture(s) are helpful to avoid pride?

dj martin

FOCUS 7

*Obey God*_____

God's Concern

- NEHEMIAH 9:16-17 *They and our fathers dealt proudly, and hardened their necks, and hearkened not to Thy commandments, and refused to obey, neither were mindful of Thy wonders that Thou didst among them; but hardened their necks, and in their rebellion appointed a captain to return to their bondage...*

- JEREMIAH 7:23-24 *...But this thing commanded I them, saying, "Obey My voice, and I will be your God, and ye shall be My people: and walk ye in all the ways that I have commanded you that it may be well unto you."*

  But they hearkened not, nor inclined their ear, but walked in the counsels and in the imagination of their evil heart, and went backward, and not forward.

God's Response

- DEUTERONOMY 11:27 *A blessing, if ye obey the commandments of the LORD your God, which I command you this day:*

- DEUTERONOMY 11:28 *And a curse, if ye will not obey the commandments of the LORD your God, but turn aside out of the way which I command you this day, to go after other gods, which ye have not known.*

- 1SAMUEL 12:14-15 *If ye will fear the LORD, and serve Him, and obey His voice, and not rebel against the commandment of the LORD, then shall both ye and also the king that reigneth over you continue following the LORD your God: But if ye will not obey the voice of the LORD, but rebel against the commandment of the LORD, then shall the hand of the LORD be against you...*

- JOB 36:11 *If they obey and serve Him, they shall spend their days in prosperity, and their years in pleasures.*

- JEREMIAH 12:17 *"But if they do not obey, I will utterly pluck up and destroy that nation," [says] the LORD.*

- JEREMIAH 26:13 *Therefore now amend your ways and your doings, and obey the voice of the LORD your God; and the LORD will repent Him of the evil that He hath pronounced against you.*

God's Will

- DEUTERONOMY 27:10...*Therefore obey the voice of the LORD thy God, and do His commandments and His statutes...*

- DEUTERONOMY 30:2 *Return to the LORD thy God and Obey His voice, according to all that I command thee this day, thou and thy children, with all thine heart, and with all thy soul.*

- 1SAMUEL 15:22 ...*Hath the LORD as great delight in burnt offerings and sacrifices, as in obeying the voice of the LORD? Behold, to obey is better than sacrifice...*

- PSALM 119:67 *Before I was [disciplined] I went astray: but now have I kept Thy word.*

- PROVERBS 7:1-3 *My son,*
    1. *Keep My words...*
    2. *Keep My commandments, and live,*
    3. *And My law as the apple of your eye.*
    4. *Bind them upon thy fingers,*
    5. *Write them upon the table of [your] heart.*

- JEREMIAH 38:20...*Obey; I beseech thee, the voice of the LORD, which I speak unto thee: so it shall be well unto thee, and thy soul shall live.*

- ACTS 5:29 *Peter and the other apostles answered and said; "We ought to obey God rather than men."*

Unfortunately, many times we find ourselves obeying the dictates of the ungodly world rather than God. We flock to innumerable 'Positive Thinking' conferences, 'Self-Help' groups and 'How-To-Be Successful' seminars, but how often do we measure their advice against the true Word and/or commandments of the Lord?

There is always someone ready with a scheme to bypass the law. I have no doubt that before the crafty and cunning approaches with devilish schemes; God has already given clear instructions. I can't tell you how many times after 'falling on my face'; I have had to say to myself; "I should have obeyed God instead of listening to that man or that woman."

Let's face it; we are 'children of Eve'.

I remember a time when I needed finances. God told me what to do, but somebody told me of another way. Failing to discern, foolishly I thought it was wisdom. Needless to say their way failed and I had to go back and do things God's way. Listening to the voices of others rather than God, greatly delayed my victory. I felt like someone had given me a kick in the gut. I finally got tired of that and decided to listen carefully to God and strive to obey His will.

There have been too many times that God has given me clear instructions, but I always had a "better idea," because the world has always done it my way. My way always led to embarrassing failure. I can't say that I am completely cured, but I'm determined to be more discerning and obey Him rather than man. It just saves a lot of time, headaches and heartaches.

I'm a firm believer that God's way is best.

Obeying God, without hesitation, should be resolute. The successful and victorious people written about in the Bible, all had several things in common: they obeyed God and because they were obedient; God was with them, exalted them, and He gave them the treasures of their enemies.

It's a good thing to obey God!

It could be that victory is not being experienced, because of disobedience. Just because the world made sin lawful or acceptable, doesn't mean that His children should actively participate in sin (infanticide for example).

If we fall for living a lifestyle of disobedience and not walking in the Word or not obeying the Word of God, then our destiny will be as those who are not followers of Christ. Destruction and defeat will be our meat, and those who obey Him will feast upon the treasures God will take from us.

What has God told you to do? Why do you hesitate? It may not be what the world is doing or the way the world is doing it, but the power of the world is limited to what God will allow. The power of the mighty God, covering His obedient children, is limitless.

We should focus on obeying the voice of the Lord. I like the way Jeremiah put it, "[Please] obey the voice of the Lord (Jeremiah 26:13)!" However, we cannot obey God if we don't recognize His voice or His Word. We have to study and meditate on His Word and talk with Him so that we can be discerning and able to distinguish between His voice and that of the devil or the world.

With the help of the Holy Spirit, we will be consistently obedient to God and His Word. Having resolved to obey God, may we be discerning and experience exceedingly abundant victory, loving relationships, health and well-being and prosperity according to the promises of God.

Allow Christ to be LORD and diligently seek to be known as His obedient servant.

"Thy word have I hid in mine heart, that I might not sin against Thee." PSALM 119:11

Reflection

1. Do you struggle to obey God?

2. What Scriptures show God's value for obedience?

3. What prevents you from obeying God?

4. Why is obedience to God important to your life?

5. Have you recently experienced God's blessing after you obeyed Him?

6. Have you observed the consequence of disobeying God?

7. What Scripture(s) motivate you to obey God?

dj martin

FOCUS 8

*Give*_____

God's Concern

- MALACHI 3:8 *Will a man rob God? Yet ye have robbed Me. But ye say, "Wherein have we robbed [You]?" In tithes and offerings.*

- MATTHEW 19:21-22 *Jesus said unto him, "If thou wilt be perfect, go and sell that thou hast, and give to the poor, and thou shalt have treasure in heaven: and come and follow Me."*

  But when the young man heard that saying, he went away sorrowful, for he had great possessions.

God's Response

- ECCLESIASTES 11:4 *He that observes the wind shall not sow; and he that regardeth the clouds shall not reap.*

- HAGGAI 1:4-7 *Is it time for you, O ye, to dwell in your [paneled] houses, and this house lie waste?*

  Now therefore thus saith the LORD of hosts; "Consider your ways."

  "Ye have sown much, and bring in little; ye eat, but ye have not enough; ye drink, but ye are not filled with drink; ye clothe you, but there is none warm;

and he that earneth wages earneth wages to put it into a bag with holes."

Thus, [says] the LORD of hosts; "Consider your ways."

- MALACHI 3:9 *Ye are cursed with a curse, for ye have robbed Me, Even this whole nation.*

- MATTHEW 10:42 *And whosoever shall give to drink unto one of these little ones a cup of cold water only in the name of a disciple, verily I say unto you, he shall in no wise lose his reward.*

- LUKE 6:38 *Give, and it shall be given unto you; good measure, pressed down, and shaken together, and running over, shall men give into your bosom. For with the same measure that ye mete withal it shall be measured to you again.*

- 2CORINTHIANS 9:6 *He which soweth sparingly shall reap also sparingly; and he which soweth bountifully shall reap also bountifully.*

- 2CORINTHIANS 9:8 *...And God is able to make all grace abound toward you; that ye, always having all sufficiency in all things, may abound to every good work...*

- PHILLIPPIANS 4:19 *...My God shall supply all your need according to His riches in glory by Christ Jesus.*

God's Will

- EXODUS 35:5 *Take ye from among you an offering unto the LORD. Whosoever is of a willing heart, let him bring it, an offering of the LORD: gold, silver, and bronze.*

- DEUTERONOMY 23:21 *When thou shalt vow a vow unto the LORD thy God, thou shalt not slack to pay it: for the LORD thy God will surely require it of thee; and it would be sin in thee.*

- ECCLESIASTES 5:4 *When thou vowest a vow unto God, defer not to pay it; for He hath no pleasure in fools: pay that which thou hast vowed.*

- ECCLESIASTES 5:5 *Better is it that thou shouldest not vow, than that thou shouldest vow and not pay.*

- ECCLESIASTES 11:6 *In the morning sow thy seed, and in the evening withhold not thine hand: for thou knowest not whether shall prosper, either this or that, or whether they both shall be alike good.*

- MALACHI 3:10 *"Bring ye all the tithes into the storehouse, that there may be meat in Mine house, and prove Me now herewith," saith the LORD of hosts, "if I will not open you the windows of heaven, and pour you out a blessing, that there shall not be room enough to receive it."*

- MALACHI 3:11 *"And I will rebuke the devourer for your sakes, and he shall not destroy the fruits of your ground; neither shall your vine cast her fruit before the time in the field," saith the LORD of hosts.*

- MATTHEW 19:21 *Jesus said unto him, "If thou wilt be perfect, go and sell [what you have] and give to the poor, and thou shall have treasure in heaven; and come, and follow Me."*

- MATTHEW 22:21 *Then saith He unto them, "Render therefore unto Caesar the things which are Caesar's; and unto God the things that are God's."*

- MARK 12:44...*She of her want did cast in all that she had, even all her living.*

- ACTS 20:35 *I have [showed] you all things, how that so laboring ye ought to support the weak, and to remember the words of the Lord Jesus, how He said, "It is more blessed to give than to receive."*

- 2CORINTHIANS 9:7 *Every man according as he purposes in his heart, so let him give; not grudgingly, or of necessity: for God loves a cheerful giver.*

- EPHESIANS 4:28 *Let him that stole steal no more: but rather let him labor, working with his hands the thing which is good, that he may have to give to him that needeth.*

- 3JOHN 1:2 ...*Beloved, I wish above all things that [you] may prosper and be in health, even as [your] soul prospers.*

At a time when unemployment is high and there is an overabundance of empty houses and standing room only homeless shelters; frequent calls are from bill collectors; the cost of energy and healthcare continues to rise; and the government is taking more in taxes, God has called us to be givers. I know that it seems perplexing that one who is in need is asked by God to give. But think about it, if you were a farmer desiring potatoes, you would plant potatoes. You can't stand over the dry ground and pray "Lord give me potatoes!" That's not faith; that's a magicians dream. Faith is when you put some seeds in the ground and pray. By the same token, if you need finances, you plant money.

You might laugh at this focus or even get angry, but it's the law of reaping and sowing. If you don't sow, you don't reap.

There was a period of time when I had no money and no job. I went on interviews after interviews. One morning I was challenged to make a vow to be a giver not a blamer. This is what a blamer says; "The preacher is a crook and I'm not going to give him my money"; "I don't have a job"; "I have bills which I must pay"; "I don't have a dime"; etc. Well, I was going to a church where the pastor was a crook; I did have bills; and I didn't have a job. Even so, God chose this time to teach me about the biblical law of sowing and reaping. Because I valued my relationship with God, I decided that I would make the vow according to my means. I started giving a quarter and strategically doubling the amount of my offering. Eventually my giving was increased, because God began to provide a resource of income. As a matter of fact, instead of my thumbing through the 'want ads', the jobs started chasing me. It would take another book to tell you of all my experiences of *giving* my way out of financial deficiency. Trust me; it is more blessed to give than to receive! God can bless well beyond measure!

Pardon me, but I've got to shout right now, "Hallelujah!"

Because of perilous economic uncertainties, I must confess that I have frequently been a blamer, but God by His grace has once again confronted me. Therefore I have repented and promised to remember my vows. I vow what the Holy Spirit tells me to give. I learned that the money is God's and He decides if, when and how He will give the increase.

You won't understand it until you try it.

You may be experiencing what Haggai spoke of: eating but still hungry; drinking but still thirsty; putting on clothes but still cold; and working but wages disappear as though you were putting them in pockets filled with holes! You might want to "Consider your ways!" Do you give? That is the bottom line. Do you even give to God what is due Him? Do you tithe?

Some say that since this is the New Testament Christian generation, tithing is not necessary. By that logic then God is not obligated to give to them... It is a real theological argument which those who are financially deprived don't need to have right now.

The question is "are you willing to dutifully accept God's challenge?" You have tried everything else. You have tried 'get rich' schemes and fads, and lotteries. How about this, give some time to God in prayer and Bible study; you will reap wisdom and direction. How about giving yourself to Jesus Christ; you will reap an immeasurable relationship.

Resolve to be obedient and faithful givers who give as the LORD instructs. Remember it is not just about money, though the Bible talks a great deal about money; it is about what you value and your willingness to sacrifice whatever you treasure. It is about a mindset, relationship, and the honoring of God with your obedience.

In Matthew 25, Christ talked about the people which will depart from His presence, because they did not give. He embraced and rewarded the people who gave a drink of water; gave the time to visit the sick and imprisoned; gave food to the hungry and clothes to the naked. He talked about this after He told the parables of the talents. God gave the talent so that we can prosper and be able to give to the needy. However, if we do not sow, we will not reap and we cannot be givers. If we do not use what God has given us, we cannot prosper and be a blessing to others.

Remember: obedience is better than sacrifice (1Samuel 15:22). With the effectual help of the Holy Spirit, resolve to be obedient to God and His Word and practice cheerful and generous giving more than relentlessly receiving.

"God loves a cheerful giver." 2CORINTHIANS 9:7

Reflection

1. Do you struggle financially?

2. Do you tithe?

3. Do you give?

4. What Scriptures show how God values giving?

5. What prevents you from giving?

6. Have you recently experienced God's blessing after you have given?

7. Have you observed the consequence of not paying your vow?

8. What Scripture(s) motivate you to give?

L. Martin

FOCUS 9

Hope in God———————————
God's Concern

- MARK 4:40 *He said unto them, "Why are ye so fearful? How is it that ye have no faith?"*

- MARK 4:41 *They feared exceedingly, and said one to another, "What manner of man is this, that even the wind and the sea obey Him?"*

God's Response

- PSALM 18:17 *He delivered me from my strong enemy, and from them, which hated me: for they were too strong for me.*

- PSALM 18:48 *He delivered me from mine enemies: yea, Thou liftest me up above those that rise up against me: Thou hast delivered me from the violent man.*

- PSALM 146:5-7 *Happy is he who has the God of Jacob for his help, whose hope is in the LORD his God: Which made heaven, and earth, the sea, and all that therein is: Which keepeth truth forever: Which executeth judgment for the oppressed: Which giveth food to the hungry. The LORD looseth the prisoners.*

- PSALM 146:8 *The LORD opens the eyes of the blind: the LORD raiseth them that are bowed down: the LORD loveth the righteous:*

- PSALM 146:9 *The LORD preserves the strangers; He relieveth the fatherless and widow: but the way of the wicked He turneth upside down.*

- JEREMIAH 29:11 *...For I know the thoughts that I think toward you, saith the LORD, thoughts of peace, and not of evil, to give you an expected end.*

God's Will

- PSALM 7:1 *LORD my God, in [You] do I put my trust: save me from all them that persecute me, and deliver me.*

- PSALM 18:2 *The LORD is my rock, and my fortress, and my deliverer; my God, my strength, in whom I will trust; my buckler, and the horn of my salvation, and my high tower.*

- PSALM 18:3 *I will call upon the LORD, who is worthy to be praised: so shall I be saved from mine enemies.*

- PSALM 37:3 *Trust in the LORD, and do good; so shalt thou dwell in the land, and verily thou shall be fed.*

- PSALM 37:4 *Delight yourself also in the LORD; and He shall give thee the desires of thine heart.*

- PSALM 37:5 *Commit thy way unto the LORD; trust also in Him; and He shall bring it to pass.*

- PSALM 42:11 *Why art thou cast down, O my soul? And why art thou disquieted within me? Hope thou in God; for I shall yet praise Him, who is the health of my countenance, and my God.*

- PSALM 56:11 *In God have I put my trust: I will not be afraid what man can do unto me.*

- PSALM 62:8 *Trust in Him at all times; ye people, pour out your heart before Him: God is a refuge for us.*

- PSALM 91:2 *I will say of the LORD, He is my refuge and my fortress: my God; in Him will I trust.*

- PSALM 146:3-4 *Put not your trust in princes, nor in the son of man, in whom there is no help. His breath goeth forth, he returneth to his earth; in that very day his thoughts perish.*

- PROVERBS 3:5 *Trust in the LORD with all thine heart; and lean not unto thine own understanding.*

- MARK 11:22 *Jesus answering said unto them, "Have faith in God."*

- MARK 11:24 *Therefore I say unto you, what things so ever ye desire, when ye pray, believe that ye receive them, and ye shall have them.*

- 2CORINTHIANS 1:9 *We should not trust in ourselves, but in God, which [raises] the dead.*

- 1TIMOTHY 6:17 *Charge them that are rich in this world, that they be not high-minded, nor trust in uncertain riches, but in the living God, who gives us richly all things to enjoy.*

It may not look like there is any reasonable hope, but there is hope in God. You can approach the doorkeeper who clearly has the keys in his hand, and though he is a good friend of a friend, he cannot open the door. People tell you that it is not what you know, but who you know. However, unless God says so, who you know does not help you get a fingernail in the door. Friends tell you that they have your back, but when the time of reckoning comes, there is only air at your back. Face it; human beings have the best of intentions, but from time to time, they will let you down. The only certainty is God! He never changes and He is able to do exceeding abundantly more than you can ask or think (Ephesians 3:20)!

Are there those who have jealously come against you in order to actively pursue your defeat? God is your advocate and He can make your enemies your footstool (Luke 20:43). All the money in the world cannot guarantee your health or happiness. Do not be so quick to devise your own plans without first seeking the counsel of God. In all you do and encounter, you should never fail to trust God!

It is easier said than done, therefore, it is imperative that we are faithful to consistently pray, read His Word and remind ourselves that He is a present and faithful help in time of trouble (Psalm 46:1).

It is time to discontinue hoping in ineffective friends or perishable things. They can only help, if God allows and/or compels them to. It is not wise to panic and lose focus for fear of man and negative circumstances. Put your faith in God!

Some say, "If I had 'X' amount of money"; "If I had a spouse"; "If I had a child"; "If I had those clothes"; or "If I only knew those people..." All those *'things'* can disappear at an instant. Government, people, riches, etc. will let you down.

Do not continue trusting in things or people for hope, health, freedom and victory, but trust in God first instead of waiting until after trying all others who fail to help.

As a result of our faith in Him, surely we will experience the grace, favor, power and mercy of God victoriously moving in our lives.

"Hope in the LORD from henceforth and forever."
PSALM 131:3

Reflection

1. Do you struggle with hopelessness?

2. Why do you feel hopeless?

3. When do you feel hopeless?

4. What attributes of God give you hope?

5. Have you recently experienced benefits from hoping in God?

6. Are you optimistic or pessimistic?

7. What Scripture(s) give you hope?

8. What Scriptures show the imprudence of hoping in man, riches, rulers or government?

9. Why should hope be in God?

10. Have you observed the consequence of hoping in man instead of God?

dj martin

FOCUS 10

Forgive────────────────

God's Concern

- ROMANS 3:23 *For all have sinned, and come short of the glory of God.*

- 1JOHN 1:10 *If we say that we have not sinned, we make Him a liar, and His Word is not in us.*

- 1JOHN 2:12 *I write to you, little children, because your sins are forgiven you for His name's sake.*

God's Response

- PSALM 32:1 *Blessed is he whose transgression is forgiven, whose sin is covered.*

- PSALM 103:12 *As far as the east is from the west, so far hath He removed our transgressions from us.*

- JEREMIAH 31:34 *"They shall all know Me, from the least of them unto the greatest of them," saith the LORD: "for I will forgive their iniquity, and I will remember their sin no more."*

- MATTHEW 6:12 *Forgive us our debts, as we forgive our debtors.*

- MATTHEW 6:14 *...For if ye forgive men their trespasses, your heavenly Father will also forgive you:*

- MATTHEW 6:15 *But if ye forgive not men their trespasses, neither will your Father forgive your trespasses.*

- MARK 11:26 *But if ye do not forgive, neither will your Father which is in heaven forgive your trespasses.*

- LUKE 23:34 *Then said Jesus, "Father, forgive them; for they do not know what they do."*

- ROMANS 4:7 *Blessed are they whose iniquities are forgiven, and whose sins are covered.*

- ROMANS 4:8 *Blessed is the man to whom the Lord will not impute sin.*

- ROMANS 8:1 *There is therefore now no condemnation to them which are in Christ Jesus, who walk not after the flesh, but after the Spirit.*

- COLOSSIANS 2:13-14 *And you, being dead in your sins and the uncircumcision of your flesh, hath He quickened together with Him, having forgiven you all trespasses;*

  Blotting out the handwriting of ordinances that was against us, which was contrary to us, and took it out of the way, nailing it to His cross.

- 1JOHN 1:9 *If we confess our sins, He is faithful and just to forgive us our sins and to cleanse us from all unrighteousness.*

God's Will

- MARK 11:25 *And when ye stand praying, forgive, if ye have ought against any: that your Father also which is in heaven may forgive you your trespasses.*

- LUKE 17:3 *Take heed to yourselves: If thy brother trespass against thee, rebuke him; and if he repent, forgive him.*

- LUKE 17:4 *And if he trespass against thee seven times in a day, and seven times in a day turn again to thee, saying, "I repent;" thou shalt forgive him.*

- ROMANS 12:19 *Dearly beloved, avenge not yourselves, but rather give place unto wrath: for it is written, "Vengeance is Mine; I will repay, saith the Lord."*

- EPHESIANS 4:32 *Be ye kind one to another, tenderhearted, forgiving one another, even as God for Christ's sake hath forgiven you.*

Have you ever tried to think of ways to get back at someone who offended you? Maybe you've had sleepless nights, because all you could think of is how they had hurt you; embarrassed you; offended you; or, as Christ would put it, sinned against you. Have you looked for a lawyer so that you could take them for every penny they have? Every time you looked at them, did you just want to smack them upside their head? Don't you just love their gall to grin in your face after stabbing you in the back? It was mean and spiteful, and they thought it was funny!

They were wrong and that's the truth! However, God says, "You must forgive them!"

Seriously...? Yes, seriously!

You see, when Christ died for your sins, He died for their sins too. Look at what He said in 1John 1:10; "If you say you haven't sinned, you're lying (which makes you a sinner)."

Consider the fact that married couples will live with each other long enough to offend one another at some time. Some couples hold a grudge right into divorce court and accuse each other of being at fault. Okay, one started it and said the wrong thing or did the wrong thing; then the other retaliated in a way that offended the other; and now it has escalated to 'irreconcilable differences'. The fact of the matter is that both sinned against each other. Christ teaches that if one repents and one forgives, differences can be 'reconcilable'.

You have sleepless nights; you may even have an upset stomach every time you think of or see those who have offended you.

Wow! That's really showing them...

You're sick and tired while they merrily go on their way healthy and well rested. Let me let you in on a little secret: they say that "you can't beat God giving"; you can't 'beat God avenging' either! So if you really want to get back at them, forgive them and let God take care of your enemies! Take my word for it: you'll have the last laugh. You'll get healthy and some sleep too!

Prisons, hospitals, and graveyards are overflowing with people who were bitter and wanted revenge. Unforgiveness will mentally and physically imprison you or kill you! Don't let bitterness and anger divide, imprison or hospitalize you!

It's time to move on. It's time to focus on God's grace and His will to forgive you of your sins. It's time to stop so much focusing on enemies and their evil devices. Focus, instead, on God's ability and on diligently and successfully reaching your goal, and fulfilling your dreams! Be grateful for the forgiving mercy of God towards you. Give God thanks and resolve to enlist the help of the Holy Spirit to help you forgive...

May each new day bring peace of mind and vibrant health, because when praying, we are careful to forgive others and gratefully receive the forgiveness of God.

"Forgive, and you shall be forgiven." LUKE 6:37

Reflection

1. Do you struggle with forgiveness?

2. What Scriptures show the value of forgiveness?

3. Have you recently forgiven someone?

4. Have you recently been forgiven?

5. Has God forgiven you?

6. Have you experienced benefits from your forgiving someone?

7. Have you experienced benefits from being forgiven?

8. Have you observed the consequence of bitterness?

9. What Scripture(s) motivate you to forgive?

dj martin

FOCUS 11

*Choose LIFE*_____

God's Concern

- PROVERBS 14:12 *There is a way which seems right unto a man, but the end thereof are the ways of death.*

- LUKE 12:15 *He said to them, "Take heed and beware of covetousness, for a man's LIFE consisteth not in the abundance of the things which he possesseth."*

- 1JOHN 5:12 *He that hath the Son hath LIFE; and he that hath not the Son of God hath not LIFE.*

God's Response

- GENESIS 2:7 *And the LORD God formed man of the dust of the ground, and breathed into his nostrils the breath of LIFE; and man became a living soul.*

- LEVITICUS 17:11 *For the LIFE of the flesh is in the blood: and I have given it to you upon the altar to make atonement for your souls: for it is the blood that makes an atonement for the soul.*

- JOB 33:4 *The Spirit of God hath made me and the breath of the Almighty hath given me LIFE.*

- ISAIAH 44:24 *Thus saith the LORD, thy redeemer, and He that formed thee from the womb, "I am the LORD that makes all things; that stretches forth the heavens alone; that spreadeth abroad the earth by Myself."*

- ISAIAH 49:15 *Can a woman forget her sucking child, that she should not have compassion on the son of her womb? Yea, they may forget, yet will I not forget thee.*

- ISAIAH 66:9 *"Shall I bring to the birth and not cause to bring forth?" saith the LORD: "shall I cause to bring forth, and shut the womb?" saith thy God.*

- JEREMIAH 1:4-5 *The word of the LORD came unto me, saying, "Before I formed thee in the belly I knew thee; and before thou camest forth out of the womb I sanctified thee…"*

- JEREMIAH 21:8 *Thus says the LORD: "Behold, I set before you the way of LIFE and the way of death."*

- LAMENTATIONS 3:58 *Lord, Thou hast pleaded the causes for my soul; Thou hast redeemed my LIFE.*

- MATTHEW 20:28 *The Son of man came not to be ministered unto, but to minister, and to give His LIFE a ransom for many.*

- JOHN 1:1-4 *In the beginning was the Word, and the Word was with God, and the Word was God. The same was in the beginning with God. All things were made by Him; and without Him was not anything made that was made. In Him was LIFE; and the LIFE was the light of men.*

- JOHN 3:16 *For God so loved the world, that He gave His only begotten Son, that whosoever believeth in Him should not perish, but have everlasting LIFE.*

- JOHN 3:36 *He that believeth on the Son hath ever-lasting LIFE: and he that believeth not the Son shall not see LIFE; but the wrath of God abideth on him.*

- JOHN 5:24 *Verily, verily, I say unto you, he that hears My Word, and believeth on Him that sent Me, hath everlasting LIFE, and shall not come into condemnation; but is passed from death unto LIFE.*

- JOHN 6:35 *Jesus said unto them, "I am the bread of LIFE: he that cometh to Me shall never hunger; and he that believeth on Me shall never thirst."*

- JOHN 6:47 *Verily, verily, I say unto you, he that believeth on Me hath everlasting LIFE.*

- JOHN 6:48 *I am that bread of LIFE.*

- JOHN 10:10 *...The thief cometh not, but for to steal, and to kill, and to destroy: I am come that they* *might have LIFE, and that they might have it more abundantly.*

- JOHN 10:28 *I give unto them eternal LIFE; and they shall never perish; neither shall any man pluck them out of My hand.*

- JOHN 11:25 *Jesus said unto her, "I am the resurrection, and the LIFE: he that believeth in Me, though he were dead, yet shall he live."*

- ROMANS 5:17 *For if by the one man's offense death reigned by one; much more they which receive abundance of grace and of the gift of righteousness will reign in LIFE by one, Jesus Christ.*

- ROMANS 6:23 *For the wages of sin is death; but the gift of God is eternal LIFE through Jesus Christ our Lord.*

- ROMANS 8:2 *For the law of the Spirit of LIFE in Christ Jesus hath made me free from the law of sin and death.*

- ROMANS 8:6 *For to be carnally minded is death; but to be spiritually minded is LIFE and peace.*

- REVELATION 21:8 *...But the [cowardly], and unbelieving, and the abominable, and murderers, and whoremongers, and sorcerers, and idolaters, and all liars, shall have their part in the lake which burneth with fire and brimstone: which is the second death.*

God's Will

- NUMBERS 35:31 *Moreover, ye shall take no satisfaction for the LIFE of a murderer, which is guilty of death.*

- DEUTERONOMY 5:17 *Thou shalt not kill.*

- DEUTERONOMY 30:19 *I call heaven and earth to record this day against you that I have set before you LIFE and death, blessing and cursing: therefore choose LIFE that both thou and thy seed may live...*

- DEUTERONOMY 30:20 *That thou mayest love the LORD thy God, and that thou mayest obey His voice, and that thou mayest cleave unto Him: for He is thy LIFE, and the length of thy days...*

- PSALM 34:12 *What man is he that desires LIFE, and loveth many days, that he may see good?*

- PSALM 139:14 *I will praise You; for I am fearfully and wonderfully made: marvelous are Your works; and that my soul knoweth right well.*

- PROVERBS 14:27 *The fear of the LORD is a fountain of LIFE, to depart from the snares of death.*

- PROVERBS 21:21 *He that follows after righteousness and mercy findeth LIFE, righteousness, and honor.*

- PROVERBS 22:4 *By humility and the fear of the LORD are riches, and honor, and LIFE.*

- MATTHEW 6:25 *Therefore I say unto you, Take no thought for your LIFE, what ye shall eat, or what ye shall drink; nor yet for your body, what ye shall put on. Is not the LIFE more than meat, and the body than raiment?*

- JOHN 14:6 *Jesus said unto him, "I am the way, the truth, and the LIFE: no man cometh unto the Father, but by Me."*

- JOHN 17:3 *And this is LIFE eternal, that they might know Thee, the only true God, and Jesus Christ, whom Thou hast sent.*

- GALATIANS 2:20 *I am crucified with Christ: nevertheless I live; yet not I, but Christ liveth in me: and the LIFE which I now live in the flesh I live by the faith of the Son of God, who loved me, and gave Himself for me.*

- 1TIMOTHY 6:12 *Fight the good fight of faith, lay hold on eternal LIFE.*

- REVELATION 22:17 *The Spirit and the bride say, "Come!" And let him that hears say, "Come!" And let him that thirsts come. And, whosoever will, let him take the water of LIFE freely.*

Jesus approached a well filled with water. He who turned water into wine, sat there without a scoop or a bucket to get the water out of the well to drink. There came, at the same hour, a woman with a bucket to fetch water to drink, but she could not make the water quench her thirst. She had all that she needed to get water, but she had no favor with other women in the town. She had more in her hands than could be seen in the hand of Christ, yet she had no good reputation and no one who truly loved her. She was dressed well and her countenance was not hard on your eyes, however, she spent most of her time at home alone and depressed. She thought a lot about worshipping God, but never went to the temple.

This woman knew the protocol: where to get the water; who to speak to; who to worship; and whom to socialize with; but her only relationships were secret and immoral. She heard about the coming Messiah, but did not recognize Him though she stood face to face with Him. She was at the well, because she always fetched water about this time, but she did not have a confidant to share just how thirsty, spiritually and emotionally, she really was. She seemed to be an ordinary woman who knew where to go when she was thirsty, but when talking with Jesus, she revealed that she really was not all that wise or secure (John 4).

Every Sabbath, we sit beside a fellow worshiper who has all the appearance that they have LIFE and they know what to do when empty. They dress the part, they talk the talk, they have the tools, but if the truth be told, they have not yet had a personal encounter with Jesus Christ. I don't know if they expect Him to come in an astronaut suit or only appear surrounded by a host of angels. I don't know what they expect. Maybe they expect Him to speak only to prophets and pastors; therefore they just live like ordinary people. They hide in the shadows of the world and six days a week they live like the world, and change their facades on the Sabbath.

If you're thirsty (I mean really thirsty) emotionally, spiritually, mentally, etc. the world says: "Get a good job; climb the corporate ladder; marry the best looking member of the opposite sex; have 2.5 kids; and go to the neighborhood church every Sabbath to network." However, until you have a personal relationship with Christ, you will always be thirsty, just like the woman at the well.

Though you have all that the world says that you need, your relationships are always falling apart. With all that you have; things, wealthy acquaintances, all the power and prestige that anyone could dream of; all the alcohol and/or drugs you can handle; are you depressed, are you empty? You thirst. The body cannot live long with the absence of water. Actually the longer you go without quenching your thirst, the more you might as well start writing your last will and testament.

Beloved, there is a fountain, which never runs dry. There is a fountain filled with living water that will supply all that you need to quench your thirst eternally; a fountain that has what you need to Live and not die. "There is a way that seems right to a man, but the way of which is death (Proverbs16:25)." You choose.

When the woman realized that she was talking to the Christ, who had living water, which would eternally quench her thirst, she jumped for joy, came out of hiding, and went running through town to spread the news. Upon giving her testimony, a city came alive and was saved (John 4:39), because she chose LIFE.

We know about how Adam sinned and caused death to be our destiny ("For all have sinned, and come short of the glory of God (Romans 3:23)"). But God so loved us that He sacrificed His only begotten son, Jesus Christ, to die on a cross so that we might have eternal LIFE (John 3:16).

Are you faking it or have you truly accepted Christ as your LORD and Savior? Have you chosen LIFE or have you chosen death?

Since we have been *bought with a price* (1Corinthians 6:20), we should determinedly repent and turn from our wicked and sinful ways, which is choosing death. Every day that we are given the opportunity to choose between LIFE and death, may we choose LIFE.

May God give us LIFE and 'LIFE more abundant', because we choose LIFE.

"Choose LIFE..." DEUTERONOMY 30:19

REFLECTION

1. Do you have eternal Life?

2. Do you value Life?

3. What Scriptures show how God values Life?

4. What Scripture(s) reinforces your value of Life?

5. Have you experienced benefits from choosing Life?

6. Have you seen the consequences of not choosing Life?

7. How will you help others choose Life?

— dj martin

FOCUS 12

*Assure the Promises of God*_____

God's Concern

- DEUTERONOMY 1:32 *...In this thing ye did not believe the Lord your God.*

- HEBREWS 11:13 *These all died in faith, not having received the promises, but having seen them afar off, and were persuaded of them, and embraced them, and confessed that they were strangers and pilgrims on the earth.*

- HEBREWS 11:39 *...And these all, having obtained a good report through faith, received not the promise...*

- 2PETER 3:4 *...And saying, "Where is the promise of His coming? For since the fathers fell asleep, all things continue as they were from the beginning of the creation."*

God's Response

- LEVITICUS 20:24 *I have said unto you, "Ye shall inherit their land, and I will give it unto you to possess it, a land that flows with milk and honey: I am the LORD your God, which have separated you from other people."*

- DEUTERONOMY 1:34-35 ...*The LORD heard the voice of your words, and was wroth, and sware saying, "Surely there shall not one of these men of this evil generation see that good land, which I sware to give unto your fathers."*

- DEUTERONOMY 1:36 ...*To him will I give the land that he have trodden upon, and to his children, because he hath wholly followed the LORD.*

- PSALM 105:42 ...*He remembered His holy promise, and Abraham His servant.*

- LUKE 24:49 ...*Behold, I send the promise of My Father upon you: but tarry ye in the city of Jerusalem, until ye be endued with power from on high.*

- ACTS 2:33 *Therefore being by the right hand of God exalted, and having received of the Father the promise of the Holy Ghost, He hath shed forth this, which ye now see and hear.*

- ACTS 13:23 *Of this man's seed hath God according to His promise raised unto Israel a Savior, Jesus.*

- 2CORINTHIANS 1:20 *For all the promises of God in Him are yea, and in Him Amen, unto the glory of God by us.*

- GALATIANS 3:29 ...*If you be Christ's, then are ye Abraham's seed, and heirs according to the promise.*

- COLOSSIANS 3:24 *Knowing that of the Lord ye shall receive the reward of the inheritance: for ye serve the Lord Christ.*

- HEBREWS 9:15 *...And for this cause He is the mediator of the New Testament that by means of death, for the redemption of the transgressions that were under the first testament, they which are called might receive the promise of eternal inheritance.*

- JAMES 1:17 *Every good gift and every perfect gift is from above, and cometh down from the Father of lights, with whom is no variableness, neither shadow of turning.*

- 2PETER 3:9 *The Lord is not slack concerning His promise, as some men count slackness; but is long-suffering to us-ward, not willing that any should perish, but that all should come to repentance.*

- 1JOHN 2:25 *And this is the promise that He hath promised us, even eternal life.*

God's Will

- ACTS 2:39 *For the promise is unto you, and to your children, and to all that are afar off, even as many as the Lord our God shall call.*

- ROMANS 4:20-21 *He staggered not at the promise of God through unbelief; but was strong in faith, giving glory to God; and being fully persuaded that what He had promised He was also able to perform.*

- 2CORINTHIANS 7:1 …*Having therefore these promises, dearly beloved, let us cleanse ourselves from all filthiness of the flesh and spirit, perfecting holiness in the fear of God.*

- EPHESIANS 6:2-3 *Honor thy father and mother; which is the first commandment with promise;*

  That it may be well with thee, and thou mayest live long on the earth.

- 1TIMOTHY 4:8 …*For bodily exercise profiteth little: but godliness is profitable unto all things, having promise of the life that now is, and of that which is to come.*

- HEBREWS 4:1 *Let us therefore fear, lest, a promise being left us of entering into His rest, any of you should seem to come short of it.*

- HEBREWS 6:11-12 *And we desire that every one of you do show the same diligence to the full assurance of hope unto the end: That you be not slothful, but followers of them who through faith and patience inherit the promises.*

- HEBREWS 6:15 …*And so, after he had patiently endured, he obtained the promise.*

- HEBREWS 10:36 ...*You have need of patience, that, after you have done the will of God, you might receive the promise.*

- 2PETER 1:4 *Whereby are given unto us exceeding great and precious promises: that by these ye might be partakers of the divine nature, having escaped the corruption that is in the world through lust.*

- 2PETER 3:13 *Nevertheless we, according to His promise, look for new heavens and a new earth, wherein dwelleth righteousness.*

Imagine yourself being told by your dad that he has a good and marvelous gift for you, but you will have to rise early prepared to go with him to get it. You and your dad get up early the next morning, but he receives a telephone call just before you get into the car. Therefore, your trip to pick up the gift gets delayed. Then when you and your dad finally leave, a thunderstorm starts and your dad has to drive through the storm to get to your gift. As you ride with him, you marvel at your dad, because he remains calm driving through the storm, even as it begins to hail and he passes through traffic and by accidents along the way.

When you get there, your dad pulls out a giant umbrella, carries you in his arms, and walks under a long awning leading into the building which contains the gift. Inside the building, you notice that you and your dad are dry. As you approach the door, behind which is your gift, there stands a man who looks like a giant and like your past nightmare. Because you fear that the people behind the door might be as scary as the doorkeeper appears, you turn to your dad and say, "That's okay Dad, I don't need the gift."

No matter how much your dad softly encourages you, you cry hysterically and refuse to go in. Your dad even shows you a picture of the wonderful gift though he wanted it to be a surprise. Nevertheless, you remain steadfast. You will not go in. You will not accept the gift!

That is what happened at the Jordan River as recorded in the Old Testament books of Exodus and Deuteronomy.

God persuaded Pharaoh to release His people. Not only did Pharaoh let them go, but they were also loaded down with riches. Moses led them to the edge of the promise land and at the command of God, Moses sent out spies to report the depth of the riches of the land, which God, their Heavenly Father, had given them. After God had brought them across the Red Sea on dry land and then overflowed their enemies with that same sea, the people acknowledged the richness of the land, but they refused to go in for fear of the giants they had seen in the city of Jericho (Numbers 14). They reported that it was a great land, but refused the gift! Everyone who refused to go into Jericho died in the wilderness.

Joshua, however, led the new generation into the promise land. They received so much land that it took numerous chapters to record it all. The elder children of God refused to take Jericho and died in the wilderness. But their hardy children did not die in the wilderness. They took the gift of Jericho plus much much more.

Be careful not to refuse the promises of God. Whatever He has promised you or desires to give you, don't be foolish; take it! Let Him express His love toward you in His own perfect way! Throughout the Bible and testimony of the saints and throughout life, God has demonstrated that He gives victory over adversaries, no matter how giant or fierce they appear to be. Remember that they are there, like the walls of Jericho, in order to keep you from taking what God has given you (Joshua 6).

That house, car, position or *'calling'* you fear is too much of a challenge for you, pray about it before you refuse it. Whatever the gift may be; let the Jericho experience be an example. Do not be so hasty to focus on your fears of the giants more than on God's will, power and His promises. Don't let your fears become your focus. Prayerfully accept the promises and/or gifts of God, and be careful to give Him glory in your testimony.

All they had to do was trust and obey God, and boldly move forward at His word and in His will. Those who obeyed are a testament that focusing on God's will and purpose will assure them the rich promises of God.

Have a blessed and victorious life in Jesus Christ! May you experience the love, favor, grace and mercy of God each day.

Loving God with all your heart, mind, soul and strength will motivate you to grow spiritually and focus on His will. Believing in, hoping in, trusting in, focusing on, loving and obeying Him truly assures you the promises of God!

"...After ye have done the will of God, ye [will] receive the promise." HEBREWS 10:36

Reflection

1. What promises do you need or want to experience?

2. What sins prevent experiencing the promises of God?

3. What results in experiencing the promises of God?

4. What Scriptures express the promises of God?

5. Have you recently experienced promises of God?

6. What Biblical events show the result of refusing the promises of God?

7. What are consequences of refusing the promises of God?

8. Does God keep His promises?

9. What Biblical events show that God keeps His promises?

10. What has happened recently that assures you that God keeps His promises?

www.ingramcontent.com/pod-product-compliance
Lightning Source LLC
LaVergne TN
LVHW051604080426
835510LV00020B/3118